Trendy Jewelry

for the Crafty Fashionista

by Tina Dybvik

FashionCraft
Studio

CAPSTONE PRESS
a capstone imprint

Snap Books are published by Capstone Press,
151 Good Counsel Drive, P.O. Box 669, Mankato, Minnesota 56002.
www.capstonepub.com

 Books published by Capstone Press are manufactured with paper
containing at least 10 percent post-consumer waste.

Library of Congress Cataloging-in-Publication Data
Dybvik, Tina.
  Trendy jewelry for the crafty fashionista / by Tina Dybvik.
    p. cm. — (Snap books. Fashion craft studio)
  Includes bibliographical references and index.
  Summary: "Step-by-step instructions for bracelets, necklaces, earrings, and other jewelry crafts made from repurposed
materials"—Provided by publisher.
  ISBN 978-1-4296-6549-0 (library binding)
  1. Jewelry making—Juvenile literature. 2. Salvage (Waste, etc.)—Juvenile literature. 3. Handicraft for girls—Juvenile
literature. I. Title. II. Series.

  TT212.D92 2012
  745.594'2—dc22   2011007407

Editor: Mari Bolte
Designer: Heidi Thompson
Photo Stylist: Sarah Schuette
Project Production: Marcy Morin
Production Specialist: Laura Manthe

Photo Credits:
all photos by Capstone Studio/Karon Dubke, Shutterstock: yienkeat (design element)

Capstone would like to thank Roxanne Guenther for her help in producing the projects in this book.

Printed in the United States of America in North Mankato, Minnesota.
032011   006110CGF11

Table of

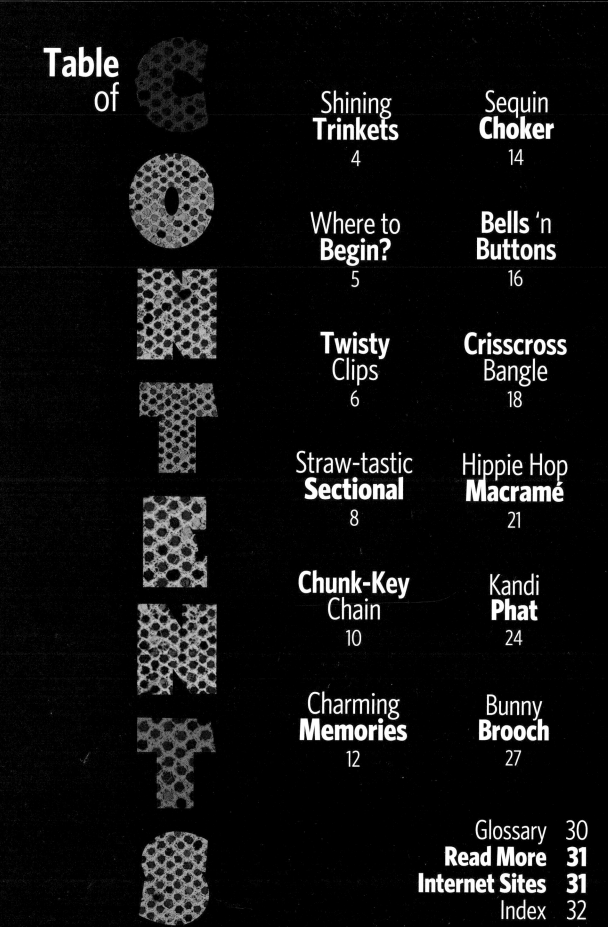

Shining Trinkets

New jewelry is an easy way to update your look. Choose accessories that keep your style fresh. Add a bracelet, necklace, pendant, or simple ring to change up an outfit and show your stuff. You can wear a different piece every day, or choose one favorite piece as a signature item. Stick with your wardrobe colors or try the latest trends.

The directions in this book are only ideas. Don't worry if you can't find the beads and buttons shown. Let your inner designer create one-of-a-kind jewelry. Craft it for fun. Wear it like art. Then share your designs with family and friends.

accessory—something that goes with your clothes

Where to Begin?

Smart fashion keeps costs low and style high. With just a few dollars and a good imagination, these custom jewels are yours to create. Most materials you'll need are already in your home. The rest are sold at craft stores, thrift shops, or garage sales.

It's easy to change measurements to metric! Just use this chart.

To change	into	multiply by
inches	centimeters	2.54
inches	millimeters	25.4
feet	meters	.305
yards	meters	.914

Twisty Clips

Wearing expensive rings shows you want the best, but losing them is hard on your wallet. Use paper clips to get that same shine. Reclaim mislaid metal for a one-of-a-kind ring. Fashion is most fun when it's worry free.

You Will Need:

2 large paper clips
wooden stick or dowel about the
    same thickness as your finger
2 beads

Step one:
Straighten the paper clips as best you can.

Step two:
Bend each clip once around the dowel to form a circle.

Tip: Slip an old ring over the dowel to make sure the dowel is the right size before you begin.

Step three:

Overlap the ends of the paperclips. Twist and loop the ends around each other to connect the clips.

Step four:

Twist the ends in an abstract design on the top of your ring.

Step five:

Try on the ring to adjust the size and design balance.

Step six:

Slide the beads onto one or two of the longer ends.

Step seven:

Loop the ends of the clips to secure the beads. Tuck the sharp ends toward the center of the loops.

Tip: Use pliers to help bend and tuck the ends to create a smoother design.

Straw-tastic Sectional

Straws aren't just for sipping soda. It's easy to turn something so simple into a stylish accessory. These light and bright bracelets will help you stand out even after you leave the food court.

You Will Need:

ruler

scissors

10 to 12 inches cord,
   any kind

plastic straws in
   various colors

hole punch

40–50 clear
   gemstone beads

Step one:

Measure and cut a length of cord long enough to slip on and off over your hand. Add 2 inches for slack.

Tip: Hole punches come in all shapes and sizes! Mix it up to make your bracelet stand out.

Step two:
Cut the straws into links ½ inch long.

Step three:

Gently flatten the straw pieces. Punch holes into the middle of the straws.

Step four:
Alternate threading straws and gemstones onto cord.

Step five:
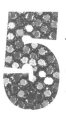
Tie the ends of the cord in a knot. Trim the excess cord.

❋ Variations:
- Dip the ends of the straws in glue and then into glitter.
- Cut the straws into varying sizes for a more dramatic look.

Chunk-Key Chain

When linked, rings stand for unity. Unite your outfit by turning
these solid circles into a bold statement. Dress up
a casual outfit or take a formal dress to the
next level with this chic necklace.

You Will Need:

- key rings in
  - assorted sizes
- small round
  - jump rings
- staple remover

- 12–24 inches light steel
  - chain from hardware
  - or craft store
- small beads
- clasp
- large decorative pin

Step one:

Arrange the key rings and
jump rings in the desired
pattern. Use the small
rings as spacers between
the large rings.

Tip: Placing the largest
key ring at the center of the
necklace will add balance.

 **Step two:**
Use the staple remover to open
the key rings. Place the points
of the staple remover in the
grooves of the ring, and then
press down. Connect the jump
rings to the key rings.

 **Step three:**
Make the necklace the desired
length by connecting the light
chain to the rings. Decorate
jump rings with small beads.

 Step four:
Connect clasp to the
end of the light chain.

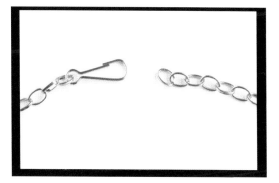

 **Step five:**
Add pin to decorate the
center of the necklace.

✳ *Variation:*
• Alternate short lengths of chain
  with the key rings for a more
  streamlined look.

chic—a fashionable style

Charming Memories

Some objects hold special meaning. Remember that Friends Forever necklace your BFF bought in elementary school? Or how about the key to your childhood diary? Think of those guitar picks you bought when you first learned to play. Why keep your trinkets hidden? Turn tiny treasures into wearable earring keepsakes.

You Will Need:

small jump rings
charms or other small keepsakes
    with pre-made holes
beads
needlenose pliers
surgical steel earring wires

Step one:
Thread a jump ring through the charm's top hole.

Tip: Many earring wires are reusable. You might have a set at home. Just give them a quick wipe with rubbing alcohol. New wires can be found at jewelry and craft stores.

keepsake—something kept for a memory

Step two:
Attach charm to the earring loops.

Step three:
Twist the wire to fasten. Close jump ring.

Step four:
Continue adding charms by using more jump rings. Add beads to accent the charm, if desired.

Step five:
Repeat steps 1-4 to make a second earring.

Tip: If your charm doesn't have pre-made holes, use soft craft wire to attach it. Wrap the wire around the charm like a present. First wrap the wire around the top of the charm. Cross the wire underneath. Bring the wire back up to the top and then twist. Trim the wire ends with clippers.

Sequin Choker

Wear some sparkle and shine when you're out with friends. Stand out in a crowd wherever you are. Show off your style (and your sewing skills!) with this bedazzling choker.

You Will Need:

measuring tape

scissors

1-inch-wide grosgrain ribbon

needle and thread

toggle clasp

craft glue

silver sequins

large, lightweight jewel

Step one:

Measure the length around your neck. Add 1 inch to the measurement. Cut a piece of ribbon the same length.

Step two:

Sew one part of the clasp to one end of the ribbon. Sew the other part of the clasp to the other end. See page 28 for sewing tips.

Step three:

Fold a ¼-inch piece of the ribbon under each part of the clasp. Sew flat.

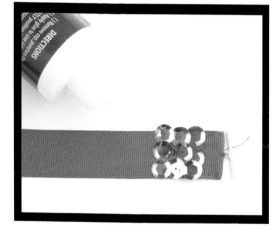

Step four:

Glue sequins onto the ribbon in rows, overlapping slightly. Avoid gluing sequins at the very edges of the choker. This will make taking the necklace on and off easier. Continue until the ribbon is covered.

Tip: Use the ridges on the ribbon as a guide to glue your sequins on straight.

Step five:

Sew the jewel to the very center of the choker.

Bells 'n **Buttons**

Buttons and bells add a playful touch to everyday paper clips. With thousands of button styles to choose from, you'll be able to show the world the real you. Let your friends know you're on your way with this bangled bracelet!

You Will Need:

16 small paper clips
scissors
duct tape
4 buttons
4 small bells

Step one:

Link eight paper clips together to form a chain. Link the clips at the ends together to make a bracelet. The bracelet should be large enough to slip over your hand.

Step two:

Cut the duct tape into small strips, about 1 inch wide and 1 ½ inches tall. Cut one strip for each paper clip in the bracelet.

Tip: Add or remove paper clips as needed to fit your wrist.

Step three:

Wrap a strip of duct tape around the middle of one paper clip.

Step four:

Repeat with the rest of the paper clips on the bracelet.

Step five:

Link the buttons and bells onto the remaining eight paper clips.

Step six:

Link a paper clip with a button onto a paper clip on the bracelet.

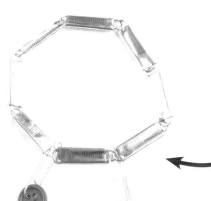

Step seven:

Link a paper clip with a bell onto the next paper clip on the bracelet. Continue alternating buttons and bells.

❋ Variation:
- For more variety, use large paper clips for the bracelet and small paper clips to hold the buttons and bells.

Crisscross **Bangle**

This crossover bracelet has a faux industrial look that blends the past and future into steampunk style. A bangle works with both petticoats and jeans! Slide it on over fingerless gloves, or wear it bare against your skin.

You Will Need:

ruler
scissors
thin cardboard
black duct tape
silver duct tape
blue duct tape
craft glue
jewel

Step one:

Measure and cut out a length of cardboard long eough to slide over your hand, plus ½ inch for overlap. Trim cardboard to a ½-inch width.

faux—made to look like something else
steampunk—a combination of traditional and modern styles

Step two:

Cut a piece of black duct tape the same length as the cardboard.

Step three:

Fold the duct tape in half the long way, with the sticky sides together.

Step four:

Fold the strip of tape in half again, and cut. Set the leftover strip aside for a second bracelet.

Tip: If black, blue, and silver aren't your style, there are dozens of colors and patterns of duct tape available.

Step five:

Repeat steps 2-4 with silver and blue duct tapes.

Step six:

Curve the cardboard into a circle. Use a small piece of duct tape to secure the ends.

continue on next page

Step seven:

Wrap the blue and silver duct tape around the bangle. Tape the ends to the bangle.

Step eight:

Wrap black tape strip around the blue and silver tapes. Angle the black strip in the opposite direction.

Step nine:

Wind a small band of silver duct tape around the ends of the tape for a faux metal finish.

Step ten:

Glue jewel to the center of the bracelet.

❋ *Variation*:

- Take the steampunk look to the next level. Glue old watch parts or small metal decorations to your bangle.

Hippie Hop **Macramé**

Use skillfully tied knots to turn this ring into urban bling.
Decorate your macramé ring to suit your taste and style.

You Will Need:

measuring tape
scissors
.5 mm cord in
   one color

.5 mm cord in a
   second color
masking tape
jewel with a loop
   on the back

Step one:
Measure the length
around your finger.

Step two:
Cut a 10-inch
length of cord
in one color.

urban—an area in and around
   a city
macramé—lace or fringe made
   by knotting threads or cords
   in a geometrical pattern

continue on next page

Step three:

Cut a 24-inch length of cord of the other color.

Step four:

Fold cords in half. Tie the cords together in the middle to make a tiny loop. The short cord is the filler cord.

Step five:

Attach the cords to a smooth work surface with masking tape.

❋ *Variation*:
- Use different types of cord, including natural twine, hemp, or leather.
- Replace the jewel with shank buttons, shells with pre-drilled holes, or large beads.

Step six:

Tie knots with the long cord. Use square knots—right over left, then left over right. Take care to keep the filler cord straight.

Tip: Alternate the knots over and under the filler cord.

Step seven:

Continue tying the long cord until your knots are as long as the measured length of your finger. Add a few extra knots and test for size.

Step eight:

When the ring fits, slip the loop of cord over the jewel's loop.

Step nine:

Slide the four strands of cord through the jewel's loop and knot them. Trim excess.

Kandi Phat

Kandi bracelets are made with plastic beads. Swapping kandi bracelets is a sign of friendship. Stack them up your arms to exchange at parties. For glow-in-the-dark kandi, choose neon or fluorescent beads. Then design a unique bracelet to thread and share.

You Will Need:

multi-colored beads
thin elastic cording
scissors

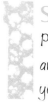

Step one:

Plan the colors
and pattern for
your bracelet.

Step two:

Measure and cut a
piece of elastic cord that
is long enough to wrap
around your wrist three
or four times (about
24 to 26 inches). Add
2 or 3 inches for slack.

flourescent—giving out a bright
    light by using a certain type
    of energy

Step three:

Tie the elastic to a bead, leaving about 2 inches of cord at the end. Choose a bead with an extra large hole for the first bead and every fifth one after it. You could use charms instead. They will be the anchors for the added rows.

Step four:

Next thread four small beads onto the cord. Add another large bead. Continue threading beads in this pattern until the bracelet is large enough to circle your wrist.

Step five:

Thread the cord through the first small bead. Add four more beads to the cord.

Step six:

Thread cord through the fifth bead to anchor your string of four beads.

continue on next page

Repeat steps 5 and 6 at
every large bead until you
have a second row.

Step eight:

Continue adding beads in
rows until your bracelet
reaches the desired width.

Step nine:

Try your bracelet on to make sure
it fits. Remove the anchor bead,
taking care not to lose all the beads.
Knot the ends and trim the cord.

Bunny Brooch

Stay cute with this felt bunny brooch. Perch one on your backpack or pin one to your coat. Make a different colored bunny for each day or give each bunny its own expression. Let your friends know how you're feeling by which bunny is on display.

You Will Need:

pencil

tagboard

scissors

felt in several colors

needle and thread

craft glue

1 large pom-pom

1 small pom-pom

1 button

safety pin

Step one:
Draw a bunny shape onto tagboard. Cut out the shape.

Variation:
- Bunnies aren't your only option! Horses, tigers, pandas, dogs, and other animals make cute pins too.

continue on next page

Step two:

Use the tagboard shape to trace two bunny shapes onto the felt. Cut out the shapes.

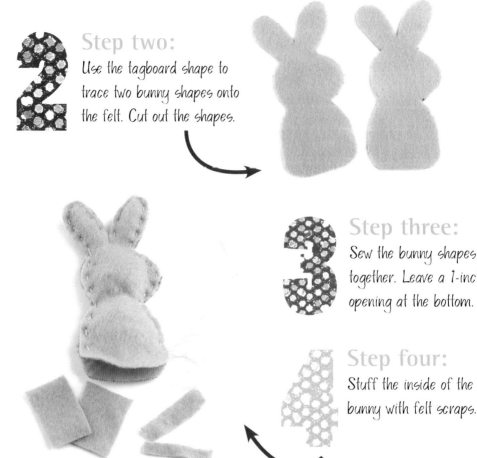

Step three:

Sew the bunny shapes together. Leave a 1-inch opening at the bottom.

Step four:

Stuff the inside of the bunny with felt scraps.

Step five:

Sew the opening closed.

How To Sew By Hand:

Slide the thread through the eye of the needle. Bring the ends of the thread together and tie a knot. Poke your threaded needle through the fabric from underneath. Pull the thread through to knotted end. Poke your needle back through the fabric and up again to make a stitch.

Continue weaving the needle in and out of the fabric, making small stitches along the edge of the brooch. When you are finished sewing, make a loose stitch. Thread the needle through the loop and pull tight. Cut off remaining thread.

Variation:

- To make your pin stand out even more, try using different-colored felt for the eyes and nose instead of pom-poms and buttons.

Step six:

Glue the large and small pom-poms to the bunny to make the tail and nose. Glue on the button to make the bunny's eye.

Tip: Use a permanent marker to draw cute expressions on your bunny.

Step seven:

Use the needle and thread to sew the safety pin to the back of the bunny.

Tip: If you don't like to sew, glue several felt cut-outs together. Use a weight to make sure they dry flat, and watch out for excess glue.

Glossary

accessory (ak-SEH-suh-ree)—something, such as a belt or jewelry, that goes with your clothes

chic (SHEEK)—a fashionable style

faux (FOH)—made to look like something else through an artistic effect

fluorescent (fluh-RES-uhnt)—giving out a bright light by using a certain type of energy

keepsake (KEEP-sayk)—something kept for a memory

macramé (mah-kruh-MAY)—lace or fringe made by knotting threads or cords in a geometrical pattern

steampunk (STEEM-punkh)—a style that blends the look of Victorian-era fashion with modern technology

urban (UR-buhn)—an area in and around a city

Read **More**

Boonyadhistarn, Thiranut. *Beading: Bracelets, Barrettes, and Beyond.* Crafts. Mankato, Minn.: Capstone Press, 2007.

Kelley, K. C. *Fashion Design Secrets.* Reading Rocks! Mankato, Minn.: Child's World, 2009.

Kenney, Karen Latchana. *Super Simple Jewelry: Fun and Easy-to-Make Crafts for Kids.* Super Simple Crafts. Edina, Minn.: ABDO Pub. Co., 2010.

Internet Sites

FactHound offers a safe, fun way to find Internet sites related to this book. All of the sites on FactHound have been researched by our staff.

Here's all you do:

Visit *www.facthound.com*

Type in this code: 9781429665490

Check out projects, games and lots more at
www.capstonekids.com

Index